ROBIN HOOD'S BAY A

A Pictorial History

by
J. Robin Lidster
(Author of *The Scarborough & Whitby Railway*)

1. An old print of Robin Hood's Bay by F. Nicholson showing, in a somewhat exaggerated way, the Village before the big cliff fall of 1780 when part of the main road, King Street, and twenty-two houses collapsed into the sea.

First edition, April 1981
Second impression, May 1985
Third impression, April 1989
Fourth impression, April 1992
Fifth impression, April 1995
Sixth impression, March 1998
Seventh impression, April 2003

Published by: Hendon Publishing Company, Hendon Mill, Nelson, Lancashire.
© *J.Robin Lidster, 1981*
Printed by Fretwell Print and Design, Healey Works, Goulbourne Street, Keighley, West Yorkshire BD21 1PZ

INTRODUCTION

Much has been written about the history of Robin Hood's Bay and Fylingdales, from geological times practically to the present day, but little illustrative material has been published. This pictorial history endeavours to show the life of the village around the turn of the century, using photographs and contemporary records.

An attempt has been made to present as complete a coverage of the village as possible within the confines of a book of this size, in order to give a full picture to those who have not yet had the pleasure of visiting the locality. At the same time the material has been presented in such a way that the visitor to the Bay will find it a useful guide to some of the many historical nooks and crannies. With this in mind the location of many of the photographs has been indicated on the village plan on the centre pages.

Robin Hood's Bay has been recognised as a quaint and attractive place for the tourist for over 150 years. In 1820 Mathew Galtrey wrote of the Bay in his *Scarborough Guide*—'It is often visited by strangers attracted by the fame of the alum works in its neighbourhood, and the peculiarity of its grotesque appearance. The road to it is by no means good for carriages, on this account therefore, and also from its distance, *it is usually visited by gentlemen only*'!

In earlier times the village and the surrounding area of Fylingdales, because of its geographical isolation and poor roads, was very much a closed community. Many of the inhabitants were direct descendants of the original Viking raiders who settled here to farm and fish. For practically all its needs the community was entirely self sufficient.

Eventually the village grew in size and became a more important place than either Whitby or Scarborough. It even figured on an old Dutch chart of 1586, which showed the town marked with a compass course and distance from Rotterdam. Fishing was the most important industry and Mathew Galtrey noted that: 'The quantity of fish which is dried at Robin Hood's Bay, as well for home consumption as for exportation is surprising. The fronts of its houses and the surface of its paddocks are often covered by them as they are spread to dry.' The industry was then at its height with 45 boats and 130 fishermen.

Later, despite poor communication, the tourists increasingly ventured into the Bay. In 1798 Thomas Hinderwell wrote in his *History and Antiquities of Scarborough* that 'the road to it is stony and uneven over a dreary barren moor and the hill at Stoupebrow is impracticable for a carriage. On descending this hill from the moor to the sands at Robin Hood's Bay the road passes the Alum works where the curiosity of the traveller is gratified with a view of these immense mountains of Alum-stone from which the salt is extracted; and the interior works are worthy of observation. The road from the Alum works to the village is along the sandy beach close under a high steep cliff (between Stoupe Beck and Mill Beck) to which the sea flows as the tide advances, and the passage is unsafe except there be a spacious area of sand uncovered by the water, or the tide be receeding'.

Old prints and engravings show part of Baytown as being perched on an astoundingly high cliff and it is generally accepted that this is to a large extent the artists' romantic exaggeration (see title page). However in 1780, part of King Street, which was the main road down into the village, fell, with many cottages on the seaward side, down the cliff. It is interesting therefore to know that Thomas Hinderwell wrote, in 1798, that 'the village once made a grotesque appearance, the houses being strangely scattered over the face of a steep cliff and some of them hanging in an awful manner on the projecting ledges of the precipice. But this place has lately sustained a great alteration by the falling of the Cliff in consequence of which the projecting houses and the pavement of the principal street, as far as the fronts of the houses on the opposite side, are ruined and a new road has been made from the landing place through the interior part of the Town'. As Thomas Hinderwell, one of the earliest local historians, was born in 1744 it is likely that he had visited the Bay before the cliff fall of 1780 and that his description is one taken from personal observation and not from an old print.

Undoubtedly losing much of its 'grotesque appearance' the village nevertheless continued to attract visitors and in 1847 in *Theakstons Guide to Scarborough* a 'lively tourist' is quoted as describing Robin Hood's Bay as follows, 'No place of human abode can be conceived more wild in its appearance than this village, where the tidy little edifices of the fishermen are perched, like the nests of seagulls, among the cliffs. The communication from one street to another, in some places, is so entirely cut off, that access is obtained by a plank bridge thrown over a gully [this may well refer to the aftermath of 1780]. Every individual dwelling is characteristic of the neatness of a seafaring proprietor—him whom early habit has taught the true principles of the economy of space and to whom the contrast of rough and perilous hours abroad the more endears the delights of home'.

In 1885 the opening of the railway brought about many changes not the least of which was the building of the Mount Pleasant estate at the top of Bay Bank. In 1894 the fifty-two plots of land were advertised as being 'splendid Sites close to the sea for the erection of superior Villa Residences or High Class Boarding or Lodging Houses'. Many were so developed as can be seen today but some also became homes for retired master mariners, many of whom aspired to a 'superior' house, with more space, at the top of the Bank.

Slowly life in the village changed, although by comparison with other parts of the country which had been transformed by the industrial revolution, it was an almost imperceptible change. Many thousands of visitors came, via the railway, and provided another source of income at a time when the fishing industry was well into a decline. By 1914 there were only two families fishing in the Bay. The growth of offshore fishing with trawlers and other powered craft from Whitby, and the lack of a harbour suitable for such boats, made fishing from the local cobles unprofitable. The First World War took away many able-bodied men and reduced the tourist trade. Families moved away and cottages fell into disrepair and decay, and the village itself declined. Somehow the community and its spirit survived and, despite economies and hardship, there was optimism for better times to come.

Eventually, conditions improved and the tourists came back in even greater numbers, not only to visit but to buy up empty and derelict cottages to use as holiday homes. These were carefully restored and preserved and considerable amounts of money spent on them, much of it, though not all, in a sympathetic manner which did not destroy the atmosphere of the old village. Perhaps if it was not for this many of the cottages in the village would have been condemned and demolished and Robin Hood's Bay as it was would just be a memory and a few photographs and not, as it is, a thriving community with a very tangible history.

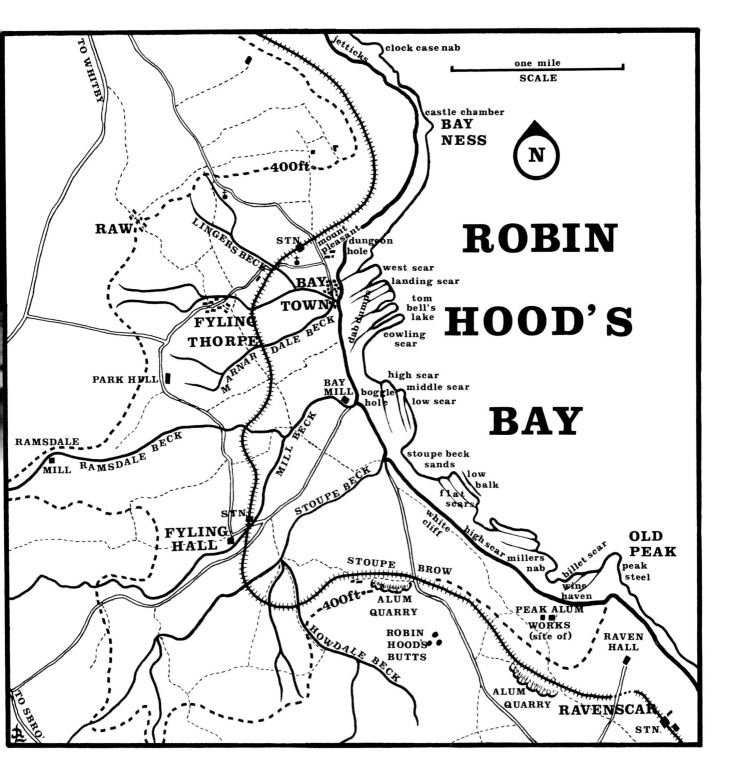

one mile
SCALE

2. Robin Hood's Bay has, until comparatively recently in historical terms, been a very closed community. This in no small way is due to its geographical isolation, as seen here, surrounded by hills on the north, west, and south sides, with extensive, practically unpopulated moorland stretching away beyond.

The map shows some of the main features of the area, as they appeared in about 1900. The names of the rocks exposed at low tide are quite fascinating. Many of the features have not changed—particularly the alum quarries at Stoupe Brow and Ravenscar which stand out clearly when viewed from Bay Town. The most important change was the loss of the railway which closed in 1965. The trackbed was bought by Scarborough Borough Council in 1975 and has been opened as a public footpath and bridleway. The richly varied scenery on this walk between Robin Hood's Bay and Ravenscar, make it a valuable amenity in one of the most beautiful areas of the Yorkshire coast.

3

3. *Above:* Bay Town from the north cliffs. The Stoupe Brow Alum quarries, tourist attractions of the eighteenth century, can be seen at the top left. These quarries closed in 1817 whilst the Peak Alum Works continued production until 1864. The open area in front of the cottages (see below) was used for drying washing as space was very limited within the Village. Most householders had, or shared, an outhouse containing a 'set pot' or washing copper with a fire underneath. Rent of space on the drying ground was 1/- (5p) per household per year.

4. *Below:* A view from Brickhills, now a car park but formerly the site of a small brickworks, near the top of the Bank. On the left is the drying ground whilst the row of terraced cottages on the right is Esplanade. This was known locally as Sentry-box Row, because of the line of earth closets in the gardens outside the cottages! The block of houses on the cliff edge have long since vanished whilst Windyridge (third roof from the left) has had a third storey added.

5. Bay Town from Cowfield Hill on the south cliffs, a photograph taken before the Victoria Hotel was built in 1897, at the top of the Bank (top left). Ness Point stands out clearly in the distance.

In the foreground, on the left, is the Robin Hood's Bay Gasworks, reputed to be the smallest one in Yorkshire, and run by one man. At the time this photograph was taken in 1890 the 'gas manager' was Edward Kirk. At about the turn of the century the works was going to be closed but two local men, including Captain Richard Knightley-Smith, stepped in and bought the concern from the proprietor, Frederick James Webster, of Scarborough. They then employed J. W. Storm, affectionately known as Jimmy Willy, to run the gasworks. He was very deaf but his hobby was violin making at which he was a perfectionist.

The Village was well lit by gas and there were many ornate lamps on the street corners—a typical one is seen outside Gallery Cottage. Every lamp had to be lit by hand a job which was undertaken by Jacky Jivvy (see photograph 12).

Coal for the gasworks came by rail from the Barnsley area, noted for its good gas coal, but one resident recalls, rather sourly, that when town gas was 3/6d. (17½p) for 1000 units, gas at Robin Hood's Bay was 8/4d. (41½p) and was inferior in quality. Electricity was not brought into the area until 1932.

In front of the gasworks, on Albion Street, the two long roofs belong to 'herring houses' where bait was cut up. Behind the gasworks is the row of cottages on Sunnyside and behind that Littlewood Terrace. On the end of this street, off the picture on the extreme left, there was a midden (refuse heap) which one lady remembered very clearly as her mother continually told her as a child. 'Don't go and play near the midden dear!' showing understandable concern as the contents of the 'dry closets' were deposited here!

In 1912 the Robin Hood's Bay Miniature Rifle and Physical Culture Club was formed and, in May, a range erected 'near the gasometer in Littlewood' but it is not known where this was (see caption to photograph 9).

5

6. The lower end of the Village from Cowfield Hill, in about 1890. The cottage on the extreme right (Beacholme) was at one time used as a sawmill and rests on a very ancient staithe. Most of the cottages in the Village can be seen on this and the preceding photograph. They were built between about 1650 and 1750. Some of the cottages in the foreground collapsed before the short promenade, The Quarterdeck, was built in the 1960s. Behind Beacholme is The Coble cottage and behind that the Robin Hood's Bay Hotel. To the left of the hotel is the Post Office at the bottom of King Street and behind these two is a block of houses which have since vanished into the sea (see photograph 9).

Many of the cottages had cellars which were connected by passages to Kings Beck, which runs through the centre of the Village. Originally these were part of a primitive drainage system but during the smuggling era were highly advantageous for the concealment and transfer of contraband goods. Some of the dwellings also had cupboards with doors into adjacent houses and these were frequently used by the men of the Village when the Press-gang was on the rampage taking any able-bodied villager off to serve in the Navy. Most of the passages have now been blocked off and many of the cellars filled with concrete but it is interesting to note that some of the cellars of houses in The Dock had hand pumps at ground level in order to empty them of water after exceptionally high tides.

7. Beacholme was converted into a holiday property and residence at the turn of the century when dormer windows and a basement kitchen were added.

The level land in the foreground is all that remains of what was once a large cowfield which gave its name to the hill on the previous photograph. The field has now completely disappeared and it is interesting to compare the amount of land in this photograph with the present day scene. This can easily be done by standing on the beach and lining up the chimney stacks of Beacholme with the ones on the cottage behind. From this it is very clearly seen that the shore line has moved about 50 feet (15 metres) to the west.

In 1913 Leo Walmsley wrote an article in *The Naturalist* entitled 'Coast changes at Robin Hood's Bay'. The cliffs are composed of boulder clay, resting on Jurassic Lias Shale. In his article Leo Walmsley described how the boulder clay had suffered great denudation, particularly in 1910 when heavy seas had speeded up the process. He explained that the chief cause was the intermittent springs (the chief source of the Fylingdales water supply) and the water from the fields above, which combined to turn the cliff into 'A tremendous chute, delivering excellent agricultural land into the sea, at the rate of many square yards per year!' Thus was delivered what was probably one of the first scientific warnings about the future prospects of the village if adequate steps were not taken to provide proper drainage and the prevention of subsequent marine erosion.
Sixty years later the present sea wall was built, but not until a few more cottages had vanished over the cliff.

8. An old engraving showing King Street, which was originally the main road down into the Village and formed part of the original highway from Scarborough to Whitby (see introduction). In 1780 part of the street vanished into the sea, together with about 22 cottages. Approximately 195 buildings have been claimed by the sea in the last 200 years.

9. The lower, surviving end of King Street in more recent times showing another alley, which has also succumbed to the waves. This opening now gives access to the walk along the top of the recently built sea wall.

On the right is the Mens Institute which was opened in 1919. Prior to that date it had been the King's Head Temperance Hotel and before that, in 1890, the King's Head Inn. Shortly after the First World War it was recognised, with the influx of demobilized men from the Services, that 'there was an urgent need for a place where a man might go for a game of billiards or chess or a quiet read or smoke'. The promoters of the scheme had the offer of the Rifle Range in Littlewood but it was decided that the premises were 'not very desireable on account of the awkward approach and the peculiar shape of the buildings'.
The Temperance Hotel was donated by W. A. Smith, T. K. Smith and their sister Miss F. R. Smith in recognition of the services of the men of Fylingdales in the First World War.

Off the picture, on the immediate right, is the Dolphin Hotel which was originally, in 1841, The Masons Arms and later the Masons Hotel—catering for the visitor trade brought by the railway and guaranteeing 'good order and respectability'!

10.   The Bank, which looked even steeper than 1 in 3½, before it was metalled and the steps acquired railings. The North Eastern Railway Company opened a Parcels Receiving Office on the right in 1904. This saved clients the long pull up to the station, but what the long-suffering pony felt is not recorded. In 1911 great excitement was caused in the Bay when a motor car containing five ladies and gentlemen and a chauffeur descended the Bank. The opinion was generally expressed in the village that the heavy car, a 60 horse-power Austin, could not possibly negotiate the prohibitive grade of the road. There were numerous offers to provide horses for towing purposes but, nothing daunted, the chauffeur, from a standing start at Bridge End, drove up the hill at almost 20 miles per hour. The *Whitby Gazette* reporter hailed this as 'a remarkable feat' and 'a triumph for British Manufacturers'!

11.   Chapel Street from the northern end in about 1900. On the left T. Fewster, Butcher, displays his produce in the open air. This must be practically the only shop in the village to remain in the same family, selling the same merchandise for about 100 years.

Chapel Street is thought to have been called Lower Street at the time when King Street was the main road into the village. After King Street was severed Chapel Street was the only access to the lower part of the village until the New Road was built down the Bank. John Wesley is recorded as preaching on Lower Street on 24th June 1761. The early Methodists must have been very worried in 1780 when King Street collapsed as they had just completed the Chapel at the far end of this street in the previous year. The collapse gave them an uncomfortably close view of the sea as there had been two or three cottages between it and the cliffs. The full story is recorded in John Marsland's interesting booklet *Over Two Centuries of Methodism in Robin Hood's Bay*.

12. Martins Row, near the foot of the Bank, which took its name from the former licensee of the Laurel Inn. Rebecca and Lizzie Storm pause on their way round the village delivering fish. In the centre J. E. Jefferson had a boot and shoemakers shop in what is now Gallery Cottage. Jacky Jivvy (John Jefferson) appears to have been a Jack of all trades —he was the Bay lamplighter, and, apart from cobbling, he was also a carrier (once a day to Whitby), and a chimney sweep, and had a sign above his door which read,

> John Jefferson lives here,
> Sweeps chimneys not too dear,
> Sweeps chimneys up and down,
> Both in country and in town.

13. New Road from Beck Cottage. The artist is thought to be J. Ulric Walmsley, father of the novelist Leo Walmsley. Ulric Walmsley settled in the Bay in 1894 and became a well-known local artist. The *Whitby Gazette* reported that he was a 'clever Master of the Brush' in 1910 and that his commission work had at all times given satisfaction. In the same paper in 1919 he advertised oil and water colour sketches for sale at his studio opposite the Station gates. Many of his local paintings were made into postcards and form a delightfully colourful record of the Village from 1904 to 1910. The author has a collection of about 500 old postcards of Robin Hood's Bay and would be pleased to communicate with other collectors.

14. New Road, Bridge End and King's Beck, prior to the building of the bakery and Verandah Cafe (on the right). Probably a very early photograph, taken before the police station was built on the extreme left (see plan). At one time two policemen were stationed here, one called Cutter, the other Rutter. The latter lived in the house attached to the police station where there was a single cell for miscreants. It was not often used but on one of the occasions it was needed the cell door had just been removed for the lock to be repaired. Quick work by the joiner had it back in place by the time the prisoner had been charged!

15. New Road, from one of the buildings on photograph 13 (opposite) with the May Queen procession passing Wilsons Coal Warehouse (now Bill Brown, newsagent). On the right J. E. Jefferson had his shoemaking business here before moving to Gallery Cottage (photograph 12 opposite). In the distance is Beck Cottage formerly the home of Reuben Storm, fisherman and paraffin seller (see photograph 35). Paraffin Reub was a quiet, retiring character who had a pet seagull called Jimmy that used to wait for him every morning and go out with him on his boat. One resident recalls that, as a child, she used to sit on the wall, on the right above the beck, which was an open sewer, and throw stones at the rats!

16. The Board of Trade Rocket Apparatus in The Dock prior to a practice drill. The life saving apparatus consisted mainly of line–carrying rockets, with the necessary equipment for firing and directing them, a hawser, and a breeches buoy. When a vessel was in distress, on the coast, the crew endeavoured to get to the closest and most suitable point from which to fire a rocket and line over the ship. Once the line was secured the hawser carrying the breeches buoy could be hauled out and the ship's crew brought to safety.

The building in the centre is the Robin Hood Hotel, one of eight licensed premises in the village. On the opposite side of the road, between the buttress and the drainpipe, is the Fishermans Arms built in 1680 according to a sign over the door (see plan).

An entertaining but supposedly true story relates that on one occasion a party of excisemen surprised a gang of smugglers in the very act of delivering a 'run' of spirits into the cellars of the Fishermans Arms. A fight took place and, for once, the excisemen were victorious. During the fight one of the kegs of spirits had sprung a leak and the officers of the law began to celebrate their unaccustomed triumph. In the morning they were all found snoring-drunk whilst the smugglers and their booty were nowhere to be seen.

17. The Coast-guard Station in The Dock in about 1900. The building here includes, from right to left, storage for the Rocket life saving apparatus, the Coast-guard cottage and the Watch house. The coast-guard was formed by the Prince Regent, in 1822, mainly to prevent smuggling and it was only later that they became concerned with life saving. The Watch house was ideally situated to look out for smugglers and a number of stories have been passed down regarding various escapades that took place in the Bay: one such concerns the capture of a smuggling cutter *Dart* in 1823 by His Majesty's Revenue cutter *Lapwing.* The smuggler refused to surrender at first even when the cutter opened fire with blank shot and only succumbed when musket shot was used. The prize was of great value as the smuggler was carrying brandy, gin and tea. A handsome reward was paid for the capture of all eight of the smuggling crew. This 'industry' was worth the risk as at that time there was a heavy duty on goods like tea, silk, perfumes and spirits. A pound of tea in Holland which cost 7d (3p) could be sold in England for 5/- (25p) undercutting the normal price by over 50%. Tobacco at 6d (2½p) a pound avoided 5/- duty and French brandy at 5/- a gallon could be sold for £1. There were distilleries in Holland and France making spirits specifically for illegal import into Britain.

This scene was completely changed when Leeds University, who took over the premises, demolished the building in the early 1960s and replaced it with what can only be described as an architectural mistake. Apparently it was intended that the design should blend in with the surrounding cottages but, apart from the pantile roof, the rest is totally alien. Smooth ashlar blocks instead of dressed stone, modern windows and a new building line, which rises vertically from the wall seen here in front of the old building, were used.

18. The old stables of the Robin Hood's Bay Hotel, which were replaced by an extension of the main building in 1920. A previous building on this site was washed away in a severe storm in 1843. The stables were used by farmers and tradesmen who brought their wares into the Village for sale on Fridays and Saturdays. Their horses could be left here and whilst they were conducting their business the animals would be fed and watered and often groomed by the local lads for 1d. The farmers would patronise the bar before returning home and it was often said that it was a very good thing that the horses knew their own way back!

According to Mr Richard Pennock, an authority on the construction of model ships and boats, this photograph was taken some time before the First World War. It shows a pleasure craft decked out with extra masts, spars, rigging and sails to represent a much larger vessel. Apparently, it was then launched into the bay and 'rescued' by the lifeboat in front of a cinematograph camera. This was probably one of the first films to be made in the Bay but its whereabouts is not now known. The craft was so constructed that pulling on certain ropes brought parts of the mast and rigging down to simulate the 'shipwrecked' effect.

The extension of the hotel, in 1920, consisted, according to the *Whitby Gazette*, 'of an exceptionally pleasant smoke or tea-room some 24 ft. long with bedrooms over'. No interior plastering was needed as the walls and ceilings were done entirely with 'Beaver Board' panelling 'presenting a distinctive and handsome appearance'. The contractors were all local men — Mr Moorsom Mennell (joiner), Mr T. H. Stubbs (builder) and Mr A. Hirst (decorator) whose premises can be seen on the extreme left of photograph 13.

19. The Square and Mariners Tavern. The first school in Robin Hood's Bay was held here in 1810, in what had been two cottages. Infants were taught on the lower floor, the seniors on the upper— attendance was reported as good.

The landlord of the Mariners Tavern, which ceased to be a public house in the 1920s, is, according to the sign outside, Richard Knaggs. This would put the photograph at about 1900, as Lydia Stubbs was the licensee in 1890, and Mr & Mrs Edwin Collinson took over from Mr Knagg's widow in 1906.

During the First World War when Mrs Collinson had to manage the 'Mariners' on her own she used to leave her son and daughter, George and Winnie, and their cousin Rebecca Storm, all aged about eight years, in charge if she had to go out. Before she left she told them they could serve the customers with beer, but if anyone got drunk they were to fetch Becky's grandmother who lived just opposite. Becky remembers the pub: 'there was a big high wooden settle, a seat with a high back, just where you came in and you could not see who they were until they came round the corner. The beer 'cellar' was at the back and you got the beer as you wanted it in a jug from the barrels'.

In 1935, despite his experiences as 'mine host' at eight years of age, George Collinson went on to become landlord of the Bay Hotel, following his father. He and his wife stayed there for thirty years.

20. *Above:* Lifeboat Day, 9th August 1913; the Vicar of Fylingdales, the Reverend Jermyn Cooper, addresses the crowds in The Dock. This was an exceedingly popular occasion both with residents and visitors.

21. *Below:* Lifeboat Day procession passing R. K. Storm's Central Stores at the top of The Bank. On the right is the Victoria Hotel built in 1897.

22. *Above:* The Sportsfield, looking down Thorpe Lane towards St Stephen's Church. There is no date on this photograph, but the scene has considerably changed as houses have since been built on both sides of the lane, which has been straightened and widened. Note the stone 'trod' on the left, part of this ancient footpath still survives.

23. *Below:* Peace Celebration Day, 1919. Steam from a large boiler, filled with the water for endless cups of tea, drifts across the refreshment tables set out in the Sportsfield. You had to take your own mug to these 'do's'!

24. *Above:* The first Royal National Lifeboat stationed at Robin Hood's Bay—the *Ephraim &
Hannah Fox*—with Coxwain Mathew Cooper, crew and launchers. This boat was delivered to the
station on 26th September 1881 and replaced a boat which was kept for rescue purposes in a hut at
the foot of the cliffs south of the Village from 1839. In 1881 the brig *Visitor* was wrecked in the bay
in a raging snow storm and heavy sea. The Whitby lifeboat *Robert Whitworth* had to be brought
overland pulled by 18 horses. Deep snow drifts had to be cut through and the journey took three
hours. The boat was launched into mountainous seas and had to return with smashed oars and sad
hearts. Then a Bay man, John Skelton, waded out to the boat, steered a course to the vessel in
distress and the rescue was effected. This story is well documented in J. Harvey Bloom's fascinating
history of Robin Hood's Bay. It was probably in no small way due to this incident that the *Ephraim
& Hannah Fox* was presented on behalf of Mr & Mrs Fox's children by Mr C. Fox of Staincliffe,
near Dewsbury. The lifeboat measured 32 feet by 8 feet and was a self righting rowing boat. It
remained in service here for 22 years.

25. *Below:* The crew of the lifeboat in their cork life-jackets in about 1905. Back row, left to right:
unknown, Oliver Storm, Greenup Harrison, Ted Bedlington, unknown, unknown. Front row, left
to right: Tom Storm, Will Storm, Matt Cooper, Thomas Storm, Reuben Storm. Twenty-five years
later the Storms together with the Dukes, still provided the Coxwain, Second Cox, and half the
crew. Oliver Storm was the last Coxwain.

Launching The Robin Hood's Bay Lifeboat

Leo Walmsley described the launching of the lifeboat on a stormy winter night, in *The National Geographic Magazine* Volume LXIII, No 2, 1933, which is worth repeating here:

Most dramatic of all is a launch at night in wintertime, with thick weather, possibly snow, a wind howling from the North East, seas thundering on the invisible reefs of the bay. There is the sudden booming of the stricken vessel's horn—that long, continuous blast, which no seaman hears without a shiver creeping up his spine, the flash and double report of the lifeboat mortar, signalling that the distress signal has been observed, and that the lifeboat is preparing to launch at once. Within ten minutes three quarters of the population are in The Dock. The lifeboat house doors are wide open. Men, some in their shirt sleeves, are buckling on their lifebelts. The Coxwain, quietly gives his orders to the volunteer launch party, already paying out the hauling gear. The Dock is illuminated by immense flares, making more dark and portentuous the way down to the sea. And the women stand together in a crowd silently watching. They too have the sea in their blood. They are only too familiar with its eternal tragedy. The boat is out of the house. For a moment it rests like some monstrous, brightly painted tropical insect in the light of the flares. Then, with a terrific rumble of its steel carriage it runs to the top of the slipway. More slowly it begins the difficult descent to the beach. The flares precede it. They are carried out along the two reefs which at half tide offer a comparatively smooth stretch of water inside the bar. With all hands now to the hawsers the boat is dragged until at last its carriage is half submerged. The crew climbs in. There is the rattle of oars being taken up then the shout from the Coxwain 'Let Go'.

The boat slides off the carriage into the sea. The night and sound of wind and of the great seas breaking across the bar engulf it. The launchers, all of them wet to the skin go back to The Dock and join the crowd of silent women who are now gazing out to sea, from which occasionally comes the red gleam of the vessel's distress flares. And like that they will wait until daybreak—for even a Bay crew could not return across the landing bar at night—in fear, and hope and faith in their menfolk to carry out the perilous task.

The Lifeboat Station was closed in 1931 when it was found that the Whitby motor lifeboat could be launched and in the Bay before the local boat could be manhandled down to the sea and ready for action. In the 1960s Reuben Bulmer could still recall the thrilling experience of a launching in the dark in the record time of 15 minutes. One resident described the loss of the lifeboat as 'half the heart of the Village being cut out'.

Matt Cooper (see photograph 29) was appointed Second Coxwain to the *Ephraim & Hannah Fox* when the boat was first stationed here in 1881. He was the only local member of the crew at that time as it was manned initially by a Whitby crew as the village men preferred to remain with the Rocket Brigade (photograph 16). In 1885 Matt Cooper became Coxwain, with a local crew, and served in that capacity for 23 years until his retirement in 1908.

Will Storm (see photograph 28) followed Matt Cooper as Coxwain of the lifeboat, having served under him for about 23 years, 18 years as second Coxwain. He was Coxwain for 12 years until 1920, when he retired due to ill health and was succeeded by his brother Thomas. He was presented with a certificate from the R.N.L.I. (see back cover) on his retirement. He recalled that the toughest job he ever had was when he went out for the first time as Coxwain of the lifeboat, in December 1912. The Grimsby trawler *Repero* returning to port with fish, struck the Jetticks a mile north of the Bay in a gale. The sea was lashed to a fury and huge waves were thundering on the beach. The vessel was close under the cliffs and the rescue of the crew was extremely hazardous. The lifeboat was badly damaged but the gallant crew accomplished their object. He and his crew had rescued 74 people since he became Coxwain in 1908.

He died at Willow Cottage in 1936, aged 76 years, which cast much gloom over the community as he was well known and held in the highest esteem by every resident.

26. *Above:* The second Bay lifeboat, the *Mary Ann Lockwood*, replaced the previous one in 1903. It, too, was a rowing, self-righting boat but measured 34 feet by 8½ feet and was the legacy of a Mr T. Lockwood of Harrogate. It is recorded that during her 28 years service this boat was launched 35 times and the crew saved 53 lives.

27. *Below:* The lifeboat crew, about 1920, in their new style lifejackets which were introduced in 1911 when the *Whitby Gazette* reported on the Lifeboat Day practice: 'They are fitted with a much lighter and more pliable substance than cork, and from the testing a number of the crew gave them by jumping into the water, equally as buoyant'.

Left to right: unknown, unknown, Mr Olsen, William Storm, Coxwain, (see photograph 28 and page 19), Oliver Storm, unknown, Joe Abbot, Stan Cooper, Dicky Bedlington and Reuben Storm.

28. *Above:* William Storm (see page 19) and Gladys Dixon who is putting a penny in the R.N.L.I. collecting box in 1915. This beautiful study was taken by W. A. Smith. The fish is still to be found in The Dock—children were told that it would wag its tail if a penny was put in and if it did not they were encouraged to try again!

29. *Below left:* Mathew Cooper (see page 19) first local R.N.L.I. lifeboat Coxwain in the red cap which was only worn on Lifeboat Day.

30. *Below right:* John Knaggs making crab pots on 14th April 1914. He and his wife originally came from Flamborough but moved here to join their relations—Henry Duke and family.

ROBIN HOOD'S BAY

PLAN OF THE OLD VILLAGE IN ABOUT 1900

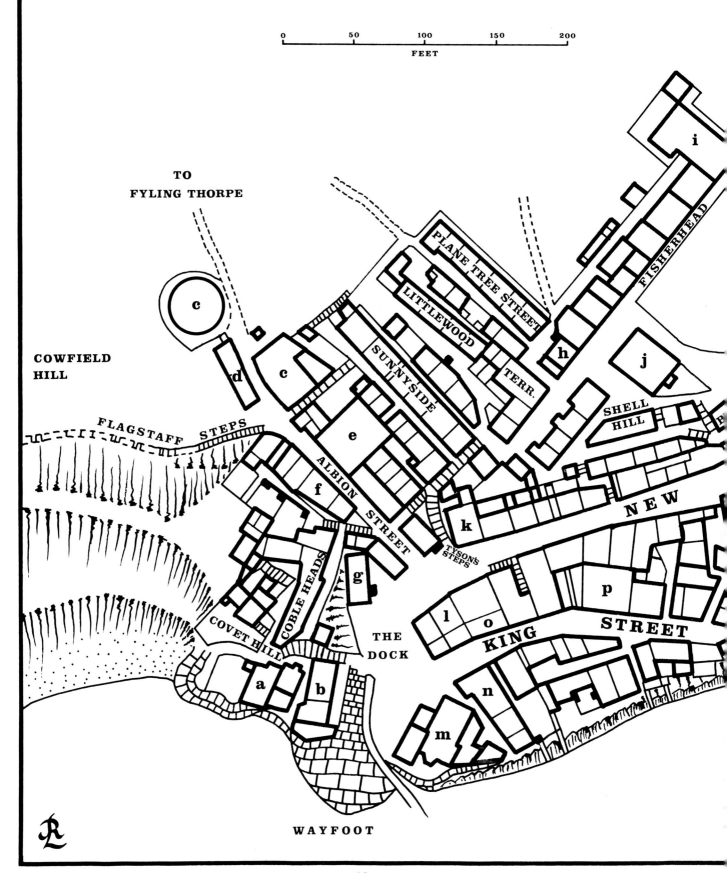

N

THE PITTS

KINGS BECK

THE BOLTS

THE BANK

BRIDGE END

MARTINS ROW

BLOOMSWELL

ESPLANADE

BRICK HILLS

s

ELLS STILE

SUNNY PLACE

BAKEHOUSE STEPS

u

v

w

z

STREET

THE OPENINGS

SILVER STREET

DARNHILL STEPS

BELMONT PLACE

t

r

THE SQUARE

y

D

TOMMY BAXTER STREET

CLIFF STREET

x

HAPEL

q

GUNNY HOLE

23

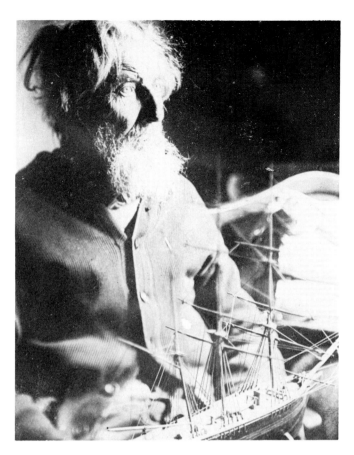

31. *Above left:* 'An Ancient Mariner' of Robin Hood's Bay, from a card which was posted in 1907. Many retired Mariners turned their hands to carving perfectly detailed model ships.

32. *Above right:* A study of youth and old age: Thomas Smith Storm born in 1831, aged 90 years, with Mamie Hirst aged 9 years. Braces were called galluses.

33. *Below:* Thought to be Mrs Moorsom, this photograph echoes some of the anxiety felt by Bay wives when their men were at sea. In the late eighteenth century and early nineteenth century they feared the Press-gang perhaps more than the sea and would beat a drum in warning.

34. William Turnbull the Robin Hood's Bay town crier. 'Will the bellman' had a bell from a wrecked ship and would tour the streets to announce all local events including dances at the Parish Hall and the turning off of the water which was apparently a frequent occurrence at the turn of the century!

He could not read and so was rehearsed before going on his rounds. On one occasion he was sent to give notice of a whist drive and dance to raise funds for the Scarborough and Whitby Hospitals. He started off in The Dock and all went well for a time but, when he reached the top of the Bank, where some of the local dignitaries lived, they learned that their patronage was required for the Scarborough & Whitby Brewery!

Children used to tease Will, who had been a sailor in his younger days, and he responded by chasing them. The young lady, in photograph 32, opposite, was one of the culprits!

35. Reuben Storm, aged 84, delivering paraffin to his niece, Miss Abigail Storm at Sunny Place in 1939. Formerly a sailor and local fisherman, Reuben was a familiar figure with his yoke and cans, supplementing his old age pension by selling about 70 gallons of paraffin each week, all of it carried on his own shoulders. He lived in Beck Cottage (see photograph 15) and, like his father, died at the age of 90.

36. Alfred (Monty) Dale the Village Postman. His nickname came from the fact that he was always whistling, 'The Man Who Broke the Bank at Monte Carlo'!

There were two post offices here, one at the station, the other at the bottom of King Street. When a telegram arrived at this post office a whistle was blown to summon the man who would deliver it on foot (photograph 40).

37. Lord Derwent and other members of a shooting party meet in the Vicarage garden. There was plenty of sport to be had in the local countryside including shooting, hare or foxhunting, as well as fishing in the streams or in the sea. Robin Hood's Bay comes within the northern section of the area covered by the Staintondale Hunt. This is reputed to have had its charter granted by King Stephen in the twelfth century although the original document has not been traced.

Left to right: Robert (seated), Gilson, Lord Derwent (seated), Harrison Allison, George Wilkinson, Jack Cooper, with the Reverend Jermyn Cooper in the background.

26

38. Captain Leo Walmsley with two wounded Belgian Soldiers on the seat at the top of Bay Bank on 24th October 1914.

Leo Walmsley was born in 1892 and came here with his parents in 1894 (see photograph 13). For many years he contributed articles on local and natural history to the *Whitby Gazette* and after the First World War he wrote three novels which recaptured the atmosphere and history of Robin Hood's Bay. These were *Sally Lunn*, *Phantom Lobster* and *Three Fevers*, in which the Bay was only thinly disguised as 'Bramblewick.' The latter book was made into a film, called *Turn of the Tide*, in 1933. All the outdoor shots were taken at Robin Hood's Bay and the film starred John Garrick, Moore Marriott, Geraldine Fitzgerald and Joan Maude.

39. A group of old Bay worthies in the Dock. Left to right: John Harland, John Newton, Reeves Wilson, Matt. Cooper, Will Allen (the youngster of the group, aged 83 years) and Isaac Storm (aged 97 years).

40. The Post Office at the bottom of King Street, with William Emmerson Russell the proprietor. This is a scene which has changed little, over the past 50 years, other than the style of advertising, and the prices! Potatoes are 1/4d (6½p) a stone (6·8 kilos) and flour 2/3d (11½p) a stone. Margarine was 8d (3½p) a pound in 1919.

41. C. L. Steel's Bakery on Albion Street where many villagers took their Sunday joint and vegetables to be cooked for 1d.

Left to right: Mr Pascin, George Thompson, Richard Sellars, Dicky Bedlington, and Tom Storm. After learning his trade here Richard Sellars later set up his own bakery in New Road, nearly opposite the end of Albion Street.

There were quite a number of different shops in the Bay including several grocery businesses, butchers, bakers, shoemakers, tailors, a fish shop and most surprisingly, a taxidermist! Stuffed birds were popular as household ornaments in the 1930's.

The grocery shops employed a number of men and boys to go round the houses taking weekly orders which would be delivered later. Housewives rarely went shopping: farmer's wives delivered eggs and butter; milk was brought round morning and evening in cans on yokes similar to those in photograph 35, and fish too was delivered (see photograph 12).

42. The antique shop (now the Poop Deck Restaurant), about 1930. The building had quite a chequered history as at one time it was an undertaker's parlour, and later an amusement arcade. Tyson's Steps, on the right, lead up to Sunnyside and Littlewood Terrace. It was here, in 1911, that a new industry was 'launched' by the firm of Messrs Reuben Bulmer & Sons, joiners and boat builders. In this workshop they built a pleasure boat measuring 16 feet long by 5 feet, named *Friend*: at that time other orders for pleasure craft were also in hand.

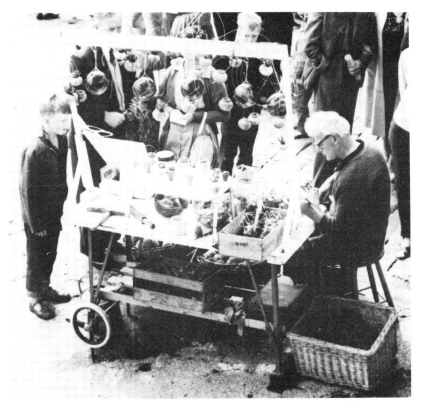

43. Not so much a shop, more a mobile stall. Tom Galvin (The sea urchin man), cleaned and prepared many strange specimens for the public gaze. He was a familiar figure on the slipway at Wayfoot for many years where visitors could watch sea urchins being made into dried flower vases. His stall was always full of fascinating flotsam and jetsam including spider crabs, lobsters, molluscs and octopi in bottles.

44. Robin Hood's Bay station in 1886, the year after the line from Scarborough to Whitby was opened. Work on the line commenced in 1872, but it was not until October 1884 that the line reached Robin Hood's Bay. On 31st March 1885 a 'Missionary Excursion' ran through from Scarborough to bring the Reverend R. Balgarnie and party to a Congregational church missionary meeting. A covered carriage was provided by the North Eastern Railway Company and, hauled by one of the contractors' locomotives, 50 people were conveyed free of charge. The station itself was in the course of construction at that time but the line was not opened officially until 16th July.

The first station master was a Mr Twydale followed by Mr George Masterman in 1890. He was succeeded by Joseph Edgar Parnaby in 1894. Quite a character, Mr Parnaby used to provide a weather forecast on a blackboard outside the station for the benefit of visitors, and in 1910, caught the attention of a reporter from the *Yorkshire Post*, 'Robin Hood's Bay is full of visitors and they are, as in former years, indebted to Mr Parnaby for many attentions. His daily forecast is published every morning at 6.30 "based upon observations of animal and insect life and worked out with great precision". Here is a sample "Wind S.S.W. light to moderate. Early morning slightly overcast but improving, later brilliantly fine, temperature heat-wavish!" Following this information there is a "Note for the Day" consisting of scraps of philosophy often having no relation to the weather. One that I made note of was "A duck never requires an umbrella: neither will you today". With such a thought as this he sends his visitors to the upper air of the Moorlands where the acres are purple with heather'.

Miss Gladys Parnaby, daughter of the station master, remembered that once a year people had to pay 1d to go along the road in front of the station (as it belonged to the railway company) but if going to the post office there, paid nothing. A policeman from Malton was stationed at one end, and one from Whitby at the other. "We used to sell more stamps on that day!"

45. Joseph Edgar Parnaby, Robin Hood's Bay Station Master, 1894–1922.

46. Derailment at the south end of the Station. Following Mr Parnaby, the next station master was Mr Herbert Merryweather from 1923 to 1937. The last station master was Mr R. E. Ascough, 1938–1965, and it is significant that there were only five station masters here during the 80 years that the line was open. The railway periodically provided some interesting diversions though fortunately there were no serious accidents. On this occasion an A8 tank locomotive is being re-railed by two steam cranes. The car, belonging to the photographer, Mr G. E. Crabtree, is an Opel, the first in the Bay.

At the north end of the platform for Whitby there was a beautiful rockery and fish pond and, in fact, the whole station was kept in spotless condition by the staff with the result that it frequently won the Best Kept Wayside Station award in the competition run by the railway company. Robin Hood's Bay entered this competition for the first time in 1912 and won the £5 Beginners Prize which was shared amongst the staff.

An unusual, if not unique, arrangement was agreed to here by the London & North Eastern Railway Company in 1928. In the event of a shipping casualty on the coast north of Robin Hood's Bay, they permitted the Board of Trade Rocket Life Saving Apparatus to be conveyed along the line on the Platelayers' Trolley. Special equipment was fitted in the signal box and a railway employee had to accompany the trolley and ensure that it was returned to the station in time for the resumption of normal traffic: accidents were not permitted to interfere with the public timetable!

47. A very early photograph, taken before the rash of building on Thorpe Lane, of the new St Stephens Church which was consecrated on 3rd August 1870. Inset is the Vicar of Fylingdales, from 1859 to 1916, the Reverend R. Jermyn Cooper M.A. by whose influence the church was built. He is fondly remembered by many of the older inhabitants and his influence is still felt in the parish 60 years after his death.

Prior to 1870 worshippers from Bay Town and Fylingdales had to climb almost on to the Moors to the old St Stephens Church which was built in about 1107. It was rebuilt in 1822, but was too far for many of the older people.

The new St Stephens was designed by the, then, eminent architect Mr G. E. Steel; a local landowner, Mr Barry of Park Hill, gave the site and contributed a large part of the cost. The foundation stone was laid on the 23rd September 1868 and the builder was a Mr Langdale of Whitby. Records of some of the costs have survived:

Contractor	£5,385
Architects fee	£340
Heating apparatus	£50
Altar Linen	£18
Cost of Bells	£507
Organ	£262
Chiming apparatus	£21
Porch Lamp	£6
Litany desk	£10
Lectern	£80

The church font, which was originally in old St Stephens Church, was lost for many years. Research and patient search by a Mr John Rickinson led to its discovery, buried in a field, in 1895. It had apparently been used as a cattle trough in a field near the old church.

48.   *Above:* Three of the eight bells of St Stephens on 19th March 1914 with Mr J. W. Wilkinson, schoolmaster from Thorpe (second from left), John Clark Thompson (third), Jack Newton, the grave digger (fourth), and John Readman, gardener at the Vicarage (sixth). On the 19th November 1911 the bellringers achieved a great feat by the ringing of a peal of 5,024 changes composed and conducted by Mr G. F. Alexander, the tutor to the band (see photograph 51).

49.   *Below:* Members of the Shepherds Lodge pose in front of the Victoria Hotel. This society, and the Oddfellows, existed to look after the health and welfare of their members in the days before the National Health Service. The Shepherds annual walk was held in January and toured the Village. A special service was held at St Stephens after which they returned to the hotel for a substantial repast. The banner still survives and some of the highly ornate crooks can be seen in Whitby Museum.

50. The May Queen and Maids of Honour in the Vicarage garden on 1st May 1914 (see also photograph 15). Nancy Storm is May Queen here, and on her left is Mary Lawson who was crowned May Queen in the following year. In her speech she referred to 'the fact that May Day was kept by the early English as a festival to commemorate Robin Hood, for it was on May 1st that he died'.

The custom of crowning a May Queen, and the associated pagentry, was revived at the Bay by the Vicar of Fylingdales, the Reverend Jermyn Cooper, in 1862. J. Harvey Bloom described the annual event, 'At 5 am on May morning, the elder girls and teachers [of the National School] went to Stoupe Beck woods, two miles away, to gather flowers, so that they might be at their freshest and best. Their bunches were gathered to the very natural accompaniment of simple songs. One of the Misses Cooper crowned Her Majesty to the accompaniment of cheering and singing, the old favourite beginning, "I am May," being the last. The Queen and her court, with banners and a throng of people, went in procession to the homes of the Queen and her maids and all the more important places in the Village. Offerings of sweets, biscuits, nuts and fruit were showered on the Queen and by her distributed to her followers. At the Vicarage they were received by the Vicar and had a pic-nic tea. The children danced and plaited ribbons round the May pole. When the soft shades of evening came the procession reformed and all, young and old, went to Evensong in the Church.'

51. The Handbell Ringers of St Stephens. Left to right: Fred Townsend, Mervyn Duck, John William Lowther, G. F. Alexander, the band tutor, and Richard Duck.

52. The Robin Hood's Bay Band about 50 years ago. Harry Thompson, third from the left, middle row, was the band trainer. The band practiced, as here, on the drying ground behind the gasworks for which they were known as the Backatown Stompers, or, when their number was considerably less: The Gasworks Hot Five!

53. The cast of an entertainment given as part of the Methodist Chapel 150th Anniversary Celebrations on 2nd July 1929. The production, which was called 'The Old Village Wedding', was held in the Parish Hall. Mrs Katie Pennock was the bride, Mr Richard P. Pennock the groom.

The Saga of the *Cap Palos*

54. *Opposite, top:* It is said that truth is stranger than fiction and the full story of the loss of the *Cap Palos* is almost unbelievable: this five-masted auxilliary-powered schooner was built at a cost of £60,000 in Vancouver in 1918. It was designed for the timber trade with a capacity of 2000 tons— about 1½ million feet of timber. The full sail area was 21,483 square feet and speed under sail about 10 knots. She measured 268 feet over all with a beam of 46½ feet and a depth of 20½ feet.

In July 1919 she left Vancouver with a cargo of timber for Immingham. She was under sail practically the whole way as her auxilliary engine had broken down. The journey took three months via the Panama Canal and, after unloading at Immingham the owners decided to have her towed to Hartlepool because of a moulders' strike. She was towed by two tugs, *Cabal* and *Symbol*. Encountering heavy weather and rough seas, the tugs ran ashore at Ness Point. A coble, manned by five Storms, T. Moorsom, R. Bedlington and W. Smith, went to their assistance, and, having got off, the tugs left for Whitby leaving the *Cap Palos* anchored in the Bay. Very strange weather conditions prevailed during the night; there was a gale blowing, a rough sea, dense fog and the night was pitch black.

At about ten o'clock on Friday morning, 24th October, the lifeboat, under the command of Coxwain Will Storm and in answer to signals of distress, went to her assistance and took off some of the crew. Conditions were so bad that the lifeboat had to be beached at Mill Beck and, with the crew of the Rocket Apparatus, they remained there ready for emergencies all night—a very cold, dark and long watch. When daylight came on Saturday the ship was riding safely at anchor. At about 8 a.m. with sails fully spread she made a vain attempt to sail out of the bay. The wind drove her shorewards very fast and she was soon on the jagged rocks opposite Stoupe Beck.

The rocket crew got to work quickly under Chief Officer Thompson but fired four times without success as she was out of range. The lifeboat was rapidly brought from Mill Beck and launched from the sands. The Chief Mate, who was injured, was taken off, but another Mate and the Captain were left on board.

On Sunday at 2.30 p.m. the lifeboat again went out taking the crew back and stood by expecting the arrival of the tugs at 3 p.m. The tugs did not reach the ship although one was observed at anchor off Ness Point two miles away, but she steamed off in the direction of Whitby. The lifeboat then took five men off the ship and landed them at Wayfoot. At first the remaining nine men refused help but when conditions looked more ominous they got into their own boat and tried to get to land. The boat was caught on a scar by the bow and tilted up at 45°. She looked like somersaulting but righted herself and was caught broadside by the rough sea and rolled over. The men were thrown on to the beach with little more than a good wetting. They were taken to the Bay Hotel where the secretary of the Shipwrecked Mariners Society, Captain H. Streeting, looked after their comforts. The *Cap Palos* was driven further ashore during the next few days and wood from her keel was washed up. Nothing more was heard of the vessel until a year later when the *Whitby Gazette* reported that she had been refloated on Friday, 1st October 1920. This was achieved by blasting operations to get her into deeper water, and the salvage was accomplished by Messrs Charlton of Grimsby.

After undergoing temporary repairs the schooner was towed out of Whitby harbour early on the morning of Sunday, 14th October en route for Blyth. A strong wind prevented the tugs from making much progress so the schooner dropped anchor off Whitby at 10.45 a.m., to await a lull in the storm. In the early hours of Monday morning the vessel dragged her anchors and was whirled out to sea by the high wind. The tugs caught up with her but were unable to make fast and as there were seventeen men on board to man the pumps, the Whitby lifeboat was called out.

The morning was dark and very stormy when the lifeboat the *Margaret Harker Smith* was launched. Within a few minutes she had to return to 'adjust machinery'. A tug boat came in and reported that the *Cap Palos* was 18 miles ENE of Whitby. When the lifeboat caught up with her the pumps were still being worked but the schooner was low in the water and rolling badly. The sea was very heavy and to make matters worse the heavy steel rigging had broken away and was swinging about. Iron projections on her sides also made approach dangerous and ropes and other entanglements added to the difficulty. Carefully the crew were helped to safety but when the last two men were being rescued an iron projection hooked itself into the aft airtight compartment of the lifeboat. Things looked very black, the boat was in imminent danger of being capsized and dragged down. Fortunately the *Cap Palos* rolled the other way and the lifeboat was free and clear. When abandoned the schooner was 21 miles from land and well down in the water with a list of 30°, the poop being nearly level with the sea. The lifeboat at first took shelter near the cliffs at Ravenscar. At 12.40 p.m., after being at sea for seven hours, she finally got into Whitby harbour with a benumbed and exhausted crew. Two kittens from the ship were also saved. There were five valuable salvage pumps aboard the schooner and Scarborough and Hartlepool trawler owners were notified of its position in the hope that when the weather moderated they would be able to pick her up and tow her into port.

For nearly two months the vessel, which in the meantime had capsized, drifted keel uppermost round the North Sea until she was found by the steam trawler *Scorpion* who towed her to within two miles off the Castle Hill at Scarborough. Here she broke in two and one half sank. The other half was towed to Cornelian Bay, south of Scarborough, where it was broken up. The masts of the sunken half protruded above water, and being a danger to shipping were blown up. An ignominious end to one of the finest vessels ever to have graced the waters of Robin Hood's Bay.

55. *Below:* The Steam Trawler *Umbria* aground near Ravenscar on 13th November 1898. This vessel from Hull was returning from Iceland with a large catch of fish when she ran aground in dense fog. The coastguard at Peak telephoned Robin Hood's Bay and the lifeboat was launched. After rowing five miles the vessel was reached and the crew of eight taken off. The Harbour Commissioner's tug *Alexandra* left Scarborough to try and pull the vessel off but found that she had been driven further up the beach and was badly holed. She had only been built that year. As with many shipwrecks on this part of the coast the ironstone in the rocks was blamed for upsetting the compass.

56. *Above:* The *Ben Read* came ashore in fog on 6th August 1927 on Ness Point. The lifeboat was launched but only stood by as the crew disembarked at low tide. Several unsuccessful attempts were made to refloat the vessel, these being hampered by the fact that sea water had got into the fuel oil. A salvage company was called in and the ship refloated on 14th August and towed northwards in a calm sea.

57. *Below:* The crew of the *Ben Read*, still cheerful despite their escapade, posed for a photograph on the beach with Oliver Storm (second from right) and Elliott Duke (third from right). Note the characteristic pattern of Oliver Storm's gansey—most of the fishing villages and ports on the east coast had their own particular patterns. This was a useful form of identification when the bodies of sailors were washed ashore.

58. The steamer *Kaiser* built in 1880 went ashore in fog at Blea Wyke (Ravenscar) on 25th July 1904. She was a regular trader between Hartlepool and Hamburg and was carrying a general cargo of pianos, ironmongery, eggs, strawberries and other fruit, and thirteen gentlemen passengers.

The passengers were all landed safely at Robin Hood's Bay whilst the crew, including a stewardess, and their belongings were taken to Whitby. For several days a tug, the *Charles Dickens*, ferried salved cargo to Whitby where it was auctioned off, sales realizing over £1000. The *Kaiser* became waterlogged and broke in half and large quantities of fruit were washed ashore. Baytown was 'fragrant with the odor of jam in the making' for several days.

By a rather amusing coincidence in the same issue of the *Whitby Gazette* which reported the stranding an advertisement appeared on the front page which intimated that:

'KAISER' PIANOS ARE MAGNIFICENT, sent on approval carriage paid to any part of the U.K. Most remarkable Testimonials, Press Notices and Photos'!!!

On 16th August the vessel itself was auctioned as a wreck by Mr Jacob Bedlington of Robin Hood's Bay. There were few people at the sale and a Mr T. Round of Newcastle was the purchaser for £116. An anchor, sold separately, fetched £3.

59. Sorting the catch on the beach in 1914. At this time there were only two families fishing from the Bay; the Storms and the Dukes. Henry Duke is on the right (bending).

Older residents can still remember when twelve or fifteen cobles used The Dock and when there were plenty of salmon, sometimes 40 or 50, brought back in each boat.

The design of the cobles (pronounced cobbles) is characteristic of the rocky north east coast where they are launched stern first. The design goes back many centuries and the origin has been traced to boats used by the Vikings in the rocky fjords of Scandinavia.

60. *Above:* Holidaymakers being conveyed from Robin Hood's Bay Station to an outlying farm in about 1900. This section of the beach was originally used as part of the only road between Scarborough and Whitby (see introduction).

61. *Below:* The Collier *Success* unloading on the beach in 1891. Prior to the opening of the railway in 1885, and for a few years after, regular deliveries of coal were brought to the Bay in colliers which plied their trade down the coast. The vessels came close in, anchored, and when the tide went out coal was chuted into carts. Every available man, woman and child helped to lay in a supply. At this time coal was about 15/- (75p) a ton!

62. An unwelcome piece of flotsam and jetsam; a First World War mine on the beach. An entertaining story is related that a local farmer found one of these on the beach and, after other local inhabitants had removed the brass fittings, he decided it would make a good fodder holder. When the authorities came to examine the mine they were unable to find it until a local grocer told them he had seen it going up Bay Bank in the back of Jack Fewster's cart.

63. One of the most unusual things to have been washed ashore must have been this small whale (a common rorqual) in about 1934. It measured 28 feet in length, 19 feet in girth, and the photographer estimated that it weighed ten tons and had been dead for some time! On the left is Miss Gwen Taylor with Miss Rachel Collinson and on the right - Jack Fewster, one wonders what he was contemplating as he looked at this carcase after his success in disposing of the mine! A great variety of things have been washed up on the beach at one time or another, fruit has already been mentioned. A large quantity of cans of brown paint once was found and some of the cottages are still garbed in this neptunian gift. Not all the offerings are welcome, the author can remember when there was a pile of rotting seaweed four feet high stretching from Wayfoot to Mill Beck!

64. *Above:* Robin Hood's Bay Girls School at Sunny Place in 1887. A National School was first opened here in 1814. Miss Laura Robinson was the headmistress, assisted by two student teachers. A new school was built on Fisherhead (see plan).

65. *Below:* The Boy Scouts with their inspector, the Vicar, the Reverend Jermyn Cooper and Miss Moscrop (scout leader) on the Vicarage lawn on 16th April 1914. The Vicarage garden used to stretch right down to The Pitts and was a beautiful sight with monkey puzzle trees, rhododendrons and rockeries. In those days, two gardeners were employed.

66. *Above, left:* Robin Hood's Bay has always been a marvellous place for children, whether visitors or local. There was always something to do - building toy boats, fishing or football, sometimes a wreck to explore or something washed up on the beach. When not playing games there was a craftsman to watch making lobster pots or painting a boat; the blacksmith; the gasworks; or help with the many horses that were practically the only form of transport. There was always something to do, and there still is though sand yachts have not been seen in quite this style for some time!

67. *Above, right:* Marbles is a perennially favourite game. Leo Walmsley is said to be on this photograph, third from the right. Among adult games it must be mentioned that in 1920 Robin Hood's Bay had a successful football team which had beaten Whitby Mission Rovers three successive times and run rings round Ravenscar and Staintondale United by winning 8-0.

68. *Below:* Just messing about with boats or whatever avails itself on the beach - a popular pastime with visitors, though not the resident crabs!
Children in the area used to join one of three gangs: The Bay Bumpers, Up Laners or Thorpe Doggers between which there was considerable rivalry. So much so that a scrap between about 30 Up Laners and a similar number of Bay Bumpers over a Guy Fawkes bonfire necessitated police intervention.

69. On the brink! Regent Cottage, in 1950, was one of the last cottages to go before the sea wall was built in 1973. This cottage was behind the Mariners Tavern and the only access was by climbing up on to the makeshift balcony. It originally faced on to an alley or street long since vanished.

70. Most of these cottages have been given an extended lease of life by the new sea wall which has also provided a new vantage point for studying this fascinating village.